The *Last* Pathway Home

LEE GIBSON

BALBOA PRESS

A DIVISION OF HAY HOUSE

Balboa Press books may be ordered through booksellers or by contacting:

Balboa Press
A Division of Hay House
1663 Liberty Drive
Bloomington, IN 47403
www.balboapress.com
1-(877) 407-4847

ISBN: 978-1-4525-0299-1 (sc)
ISBN: 978-1-4525-0300-4 (ebk)

Printed in the United States of America

Balboa Press rev. date: 10/27/2011

Dedicated to Arch Angel Michael

Thank you for kicking my Butt

Archangel Michael has told me to write this story, and that it will find the people it is to help.

I hope so, I have never written a book before. But this is for all Earth Angels travelling their chosen path. The path we agreed to before reincarnating from heaven. Unfortunately or maybe fortunately there is a veil pulled over our memory when we arrive so that we do not know our future. But always know we do not walk alone. Angels walk beside us every step of the way.

Part One

I was born during world war 2, my birth Father was overseas fighting and my Mother raised me on her own with help from my paternal Grandmother.

The war ended when I was 10 months old and my Father returned home a shadow of his former self both physically and mentally a shattered wreck. He was impossible to live with and my Mother for our safety divorced him soon after.

My Mother then met my REAL Father when I was around 2 years old, he was an amputee with a big heart, strength and very handsome. Childhood days were happy and I was well loved.

We lived in an apartment above my Mothers bookshop and next door was an Adams Bruce Ice cream shop, I was the mascot for their marching team. It was great fun.

Dad and I shared whooping cough together and during this illness the shop kept us well supplied with ice cream and this did help to soothe our red raw throats.

We moved North so Dad, who was now wearing a brand new artificial leg, could get work.

Dad knew the meaning of hard work by day he assembled venetian blinds and by night he would go back and cut lathe for the next days work.

By the time I was 6 years old a little brother was born. We all adored him.

When I was 9 years old my Mother delivered identical twin girls and shortly after this we moved into a brand new home, it was called a 3% government home meaning that the rental plus interest of 3% paid off the house and then we owned it outright. This was a wonderful start for people who were unable to get a deposit saved.

As a child I used to go to my paternal Grandmothers for one week of each school holidays. I loved this as it got me away from my Siblings and Nana spoilt me rotten. I had my own wardrobe of new clothes all very expensive, my own dolls and toys, that stayed there, and my birth Father or his brother would come and visit me. I was a little Princess.

One time when I was there my Uncle came to stay over at my Nana's she put him in the same room as me in the spare bed. I was 9 years old.

He awakened me when he came into the bedroom, and got into bed with me, holding my hand on him to masturbate himself I kept saying no, no and crying but he told me he loved me so much and this was how grown-ups showed it.

He then started to try and enter me for intercourse, it hurt me so much I screamed and screamed for my Nana, she came running and saw what had been happening and ordered him out of her house never ever to come back, she totally disowned him.

I was so shaken and scared and bleeding, that Nana took me into her bed to sleep with her. Needless to say she changed my sheets the next day as there was some blood on them.

Nana pleaded with me not to tell Mum and Dad as she said they would stop me going to stay with her. I was allowed to take my favourite doll Trudy home with me when I left, I think that Nana knew that I would tell Mum and Dad. They took the matter to court and had the visitation rights cancelled. I never saw her again, but I still have vivid memories of her and feel her around me quite often.

It took me many years to overcome the feelings of betrayal and guilt and dirtiness that this incident left on me. However one night the Angels appeared to me and told me it was not my fault and I was not to feel guilty, I asked the Angels to take away the feelings and bad memories which they did.

Little child so forlorn

Do not regret that you were born

You have been cleansed by Angels dear

So do not shed another tear

Follow your path along the way

We are beside you day by day.

About this time in my life I would get what I called my gut feeling when decisions had to be made, if I listened and acted on these feelings, things went well BUT if I ignored these feelings then generally I would really regret it. (I was a slow learner)

I did not fit in very well at school as I was a bit different to other girls in my classes. I had to race home after school to help Mum with the kids. Mum was starting to display some frightening tendencies of violence. She was drinking heavily and was on valium a nasty combination.

It was my job to protect my brother and sisters sometimes once Dad had gone back to work after dinner, if Mum had one of her tantrums I would have to barricade us all in the twins bedroom until Dad got home to rescue us.

My brother was always a good diversion as in Mums eyes he could do no wrong. He played rugby from the age of 5 years and was very good. He ended up playing for 2 provinces, however he damaged both his knees and even though he had operations he could no longer play and his career was sadly cut short.

When I was 18 years old my Mother had another baby. She totally ignored this adorable little girl from the moment she was born.

The baby slept in my room at so I could feed and change her. I used to bath her in the morning, feed her and rush off to work, at lunch time I would race home to do it all again.

We were so lucky that she was a placid little thing and hardly ever cried. My brother and I just loved her as did Dad and the twins with everyone pitching in to give this gorgeous child all our love and support.

As she got older Dad used to take her to a friends' place for the day and finally when she was old enough she was sent to boarding school.

All our lives Dad taught us the ethic of work, to always do our best, to be strong and most importantly to be honest, this was one of the most valuable lessons of my childhood.

Dad was always a shining example even today at 90 years old he will still fence, clear land, paint, whatever is needed to be done he does. He has a phenomenal memory and still drives his car.

When I was 19 years I met the man I wanted to marry, we worked hard to save for our own home. He worked 3 – 4 jobs and I worked 2 and finally we had saved up a deposit for our first home. We had been engaged for 18 months and had our wedding date set having booked halls, caterers etc. this was all coinciding with our house being finished so that we could move straight in as a married couple.

One day I got home from work and my Mother was having another of her monumental tantrums and told me I was not getting married that she had cancelled everything. I had learnt over time to just go about everything quietly not to stir her up more, I figured if I gave it a couple of days she would calm down and we could rebook everything. Not to be she was adamant she was not losing her housemaid.

I had always been on a strict curfew, even while I was engaged I was only allowed out 2-1/2 times per week Wednesday night till 10pm which meant we couldn't even go to the movies, as they didn't end till 10.30pm, Saturdays till 11pm and Sunday afternoons until 5pm BUT generally included my brother. After 2 weeks with Mum deciding she still would not let me get married (I was 20 years old) and needed parental permission until I was 21 years old.

I went home on Wednesday night deliberately late and went into her bedroom and told her that she would give me permission to get married or I would get pregnant (her biggest fear).

Next morning she told me she would rebook all the wedding matters that day while I was at work, however it was too late and everyone had other bookings. However Dad came to the rescue and said we would paint out the new garage and have the reception in there. I couldn't wait for it to happen and leave home.

Having been married for 2 years I fell pregnant, we very proudly went around to my parents home to tell then the good news, my Mother threw a monumental tantrum, told us she was too young to be a Grandmother and as she was throwing us out of the house she said I hope the baby dies it would serve you right.

She got her wish our beautiful little boy was born 6 weeks prematurely, my placenta did not develop properly and he was too weak to survive more than 6 hours.

My husband out of duty rang my parents to tell them the sad news my parents came to the hospital with my Mother flounced in and said to me it serves you right I told you that I was too young to be a Grandmother and flounced out again.

I was still in hospital when they buried our beautiful boy. My poor husband had to carry the tiny white coffin to the graveside. My parents arrived just as everything was concluded and as usual Mother needed to be the centre of attention and threw a tantrum because they hadn't waited for her.

I think if I had been there I would have pushed her into the grave.

Baby Angel couldn't stay

We will meet another day

We know you watch us from above

Where you're surrounded by eternal love.

It took a long time for my grief to abate. We carried on coping with life trying to have another baby but it took a long time for it to happen.

Our beautiful daughter was born at Easter at exactly the same date and time as her brother. Her birth was so joyous and quick, we barely made the hospital, they told my husband to stay in the waiting room while they settled me in and they would then come and get him.

Twenty minutes later they were back congratulating him on his beautiful baby girl. He said to him it couldn't be his as he had only just bought me in, he didn't believe them until he saw us both. Lots of tears and laughter were shared by all.

We were unable to tell my parents as they had left town without telling us and we didn't know where they had gone.

My maternal Grandmother had been a tower of strength to me while we had gone through our difficulties. She came up to the hospital to visit her new Great granddaughter she just fell in love with her, and said to me this is the best day of my life, thank you darling, I have stayed alive for this moment.

We were having my Nana round for dinner when the baby was 3 months old however, I had popped in to see her the day before, she had all these precious gifts for the baby which she insisted I take home with me that day. I had said to her wait until tomorrow, when we will pick you up in the car for dinner. No! she said firmly I want you to take them now. She passed over that night, she knew, and felt her life was now complete so she could go home.

Nana darling time to go

Up to Heaven now to know

Your Great Grandson needs you now

Your loving arms around him tight

Helping him to sleep at night

Both watching us from up above

Sending us your special love

We moved to the bottom of the South Island with my husbands work and 3 years and another miscarriage later our second daughter was born. Again I had the same placenta problem that I had had with our son but this time they were looking for it. A weekly injection did the trick although I swear by butt was black and blue by the end of 9 months, however it was a very small price to pay.

My Specialist told me I was not to have any more pregnancies as this one nearly cost me my life and the placenta problem would continue. I felt truly blessed to have 2 beautiful girls.

My new daughter was born with a bad eye squint and at one year old they operated on her to fix the problem. This however only made the matter worse and they had to operate again 6 weeks later, she was so tiny and it was heartrending to see this small angel go through this.

At 15 months she had to have a double operation one to widen her bowel passage and the other to fix an umbilical hernia caused by the canal problem, coupled with this she had to have another 2 eye operations. Today when she is tired or stressed her eye still turns in a bit.

Her big sister adored her and they were very close as children and still are as adults.

Life was not to be easy for her as she had brittle bones and only had to fall over or bump into something and she would break a bone.

She had 7 broken bones in 18 months and on her last visit into hospital they nursing staff questioned her about Mummy or Daddy hitting her.

She was terribly upset but NOT as upset as her parents. I insisted they test her and find out what on earth was the matter. They finally came back to us with she was so tiny and with her eye problems she needed to be taught balance ballet should do the trick they said.

My eldest daughter was wonderful it wasn't easy for her to have been the centre of our universe for 3 years and then have a sister that required a lot of attention. There was never any jealousy and she just accepted that she had to help with baby too.

At this time we moved again to Wellington where I developed a bony growth around my spinal cord. I spent several stints of 3 months in body plaster, I had to my maternity clothes to cover the plaster.

Finally after 18 months they decided to operate on my spine and I ended up in hospital for 6 weeks.

As part of my recuperation the Specialist suggested we fly somewhere tropical where I could sit in sea water to aid the healing, so heavily sedated we flew to Fiji, it was wonderful although I nearly got bitten by a poisonous sea snake, I think the only thing that saved me were Angels telling me not to move it would be alright and of course as always they were right.

Life continued on after another 2 operations to try and fix nerves damaged during the first operation. Which to this day are still damaged.

The girls were growing into delightful young ladies.

The eldest being very talented in anything creative, she could see a dress in a shop and come home and make it herself without a pattern, she was very good at pottery and crafts and today is a wonderful artist. She also had a wicked sense of humour and would have everyone laughing at her impersonations. She was very extroverted and was very popular with her peers.

Her younger sister was just the opposite she would spend hours in her room playing with her Barbie dolls or reading.

One night their Father picked me up from work (I managed an Employment Agency) and when we got home he told me he was leaving me for a much younger woman that he worked with. He had always worked back at night and this was where it all happened. At that he turned and walked out.

I was so devastated we had been married for 19 years and everyone always told us how devoted we were, I never suspected a thing.

I grew suicidal luckily I had a very good friend who was psychic and she would turn up on my door step or ring me at a critical moment, she was an Earth Angel.

Tearful days lonely nights

I fear my senses have lost their sights

Trying to keep strong for my 2 girls

Cause they suffer too in their own worlds

Work as a team to be as one

Thru the dark and into the sun.

I have always believed in Angels and reincarnations. I believe we came to Earth to live a plan we had agreed to in heaven. These journeys are usually to take care of unfinished business or to learn a new lesson, to make our beliefs stronger or to be in place to teach others.

Boy the toughness which had been before was just about to turn into a walk in the park.

I moved to Australia leaving my 2 girls with their Father and his new Bride while I got settled and could send for them. They came over to me for school holidays etc

BATTERED WOMEN

On my life path I had come across these ladies and like a lot of us, thought, I wouldn't put up with that. Why doesn't she leave? Why does she go back? Why does she deny this is happening to her? We've all seen the bruises and listened to all the excuses.

I was a strong lady with a good job, having a lovely life finally.

THEN I met this man, he kept ringing me, sending me flowers, wining and dining me and finally begged me move in with him which I did.

That's when it all changed I had my youngest daughter living with by then.

What I went through in this relationship was worse than my worst nightmare. I was taken to and from work. I had no money and became very adept at lying to my friends and family re my spate of injuries and bruising. I lost all confidence my work suffered and I was a complete wreck.

My daughter and I ran away one day and I promised her I would not go back.

I rang my sister to tell her and she invited us over for dinner.

He rang her to see if I was there and she told him we were going over for dinner. He turned up with flowers and champagne, they all insisted that I go for a drive with him and talk it out. He begged and pleaded and threatened to kill himself if I didn't go back, I went like a lamb to the slaughter.

My daughter left home after it all started again and I couldn't blame her I had broken my promise to her. In the end I sold my business to my business partner and fled to New Zealand to my Fathers, knowing I would be safe there.

He found me and turned up on the doorstep threatening to fix my Father if I didn't go back to him, I felt so trapped but I bargained that we stay in Dads garage flat. I knew he wouldn't hit me in front of Dad.

After 9 months with no problems we moved out on our own. One day he rang my Father and told him that I had attempted suicide. That I had slashed my wrist and taken a pile of sleeping pills???? He had put me in a cold bath to bring me round. Dad told him to get me out of the bath and put some clothes on me before the ambulance arrived.

The ambulance rushed me to hospital which was 45 minutes away they told me that they nearly lost me but I was a fighter and came around just after they had me on the bed in hospital.

My Father was there and I was surrounded by Doctors and Nurses with HIM standing in the doorway I started to scream and the Doctors ordered him out of the room, when I told him what he had done to me, they banned him from the Hospital.

The Doctors told me that an Angel was watching over me as with all that had been done to me I should have been dead.

Needless to say I asked my Dad to get a Solicitor to the hospital and took out an intervention order and started divorce proceedings.

Angels let me hear your voices

Let me always see your light

When my life is at its darkest

Let me always feel your might

For with your wings wrapped all around me

I can face the darkest plight

I went back to Australia went back into business and totally turned my life around. I contacted my sisters in Australia whom I had lost touch with and after a while started enjoying my life once again.

This section of my life was to teach me compassion and love for people in difficult circumstances, to reach out and help them to be strong. Not to judge their lack of strength to extricate themselves from their difficulties. Because unless, we have walked in their shoes, we can never know. And guess what I had ignored my gut feeling (slow learner).

MY AWAKENING

How do you hear Angels? It is not like talking to someone next to you. I know when the Angels are around me because I get a shudder feeling through my shoulders and a warm feeling inside me, I hear the Angels as thought patterns I may ask them a question and next moment the answer will come through as a thought. It gets better as you get more used to it. In the beginning I was for ever telling the Angels to speak louder so I could hear them and they did

Around this time I was becoming more and more intuitive, I could see peoples aura's

And I would get messages through from AA Michael, now, and while this may sound exciting I thought I was going mental, how could I tell people I heard voices? They would put me in a strait jacket.

I had met a beautifully gentle man by this time and we built a dream home in the Mountains. But he could not believe any of this nonsense I was coming up with.

One day going to work on the train (a 2 hour journey) I asked AA Michael to prove to me that what I was hearing was real and that I was not mental.

A few weeks earlier I had been regressed, one of my past lives having been as a Maori Princess I had 2 sons.

AA Michael told me I had been a member of the Te Puia tribe at Rotorua New Zealand he gave me details of my husbands death and the names of my 2 sons and what had happened to them.

As soon as I got to work I googled this so called Te Puia tribe, my Boss who I had told was right beside me. You could have heard a pin drop as everything I had been told, unfolded before my eyes. My Boss who was a staunch disciple of AA Michael was shaking we were both filled with an enveloping love which not only filled us, it totally surrounded us. How lucky were we that AA Michael showed us the light.

Unfortunately my husband continued to be an unbeliever and we separated. He died 18 months later of cancer, I was told that this would happen but it didn't make it any easier. He was such a lovely man.

I moved interstate to be nearer to my 2 daughters and my grandsons. It was lovely being so close to them however I could not stand the extreme heat and I found it spiritually barren for me.

I moved to Victoria and went into a partnership in a greyhound complex, rearing whelping boarding and racing. The life was serene we were out in the country overlooking a mountain and I loved the dogs. However my business partner and I did not see eye to eye on business matters, so we put the property on the market.

I have asked AA Michael and my Guide Theodore why? The rest of my family have all been in long happy marriages. Why cant I? I was told very firmly that this was my last incarnation and it was about completing unions and unfinished business from past lives.

Part Two

THE REAL JOURNEY

I have found in this awakening you are lead intuitively to like—minded people who are put in your path to help develop your skills.

You learn from these people what is needed and then you move on.

I met 2 of these people in the Mountains. One an elderly lady, who I met in a restaurant. She would read me a lot of Angel cards and then she regressed me (which was a bit like being hypnotised in some ways.) including the Maori Princess she took me back to 5 lives, it was interesting that my youngest sister was with me in one life in London.

However my sessions with her were always the same and I needed to move on.

One day I found a business card in my handbag, I honestly don't know how it got there I did not know this person, I had never even heard of her. However I rang the number and she told me she ran a lot of Angel development classes.

It was a bit like ET phone home she knew what I was talking about, hearing voices, talking to AA Michael, going places you have never been before, but you knew that you had.

This Lady took me under her wing and although I went to all of her courses I never paid for more than the first one, so I helped to cater the lunches as these were all full weekend classes.

The first course that really impacted me was Developing Intuition, where after tuition and explanations we were partnered up with another course member my partner was a male. He tried first to see if he could get anything for me but was unable to get through to any spirit, which was a bit disappointing.

When my turn came I asked the Angels to bring through a message for him

I just about jumped out of my skin when all of a sudden and elderly couple appeared on either side of him, a very tall gentleman and a shorter white haired lady. I described them to my partner and said the male seems to be the controller, he smiled and said that is my Grandparents. My Grandad always talked over Nana but they were very close.

I told him his Grandfather said that the decision my partner had made was the right one. Than he should stick to it, and everything would work out perfectly. Grandmother then piped in and said we are proud of you and are always with you, and with that they faded away.

I burst into tears with such an emotional drain, and my partner wore a smile for the rest of the afternoon.

After everyone had gone that night and we had cleaned up, we enjoyed a quiet cup of tea my Tutor told me that my partner would not be back tomorrow, she said she had asked him if she could let me know why, he agreed.

He had been torn apart for some time, trying to decide on whether to stay married or to go into the Priesthood. He was being drawn very strongly to the Church and had just made the decision to tell his wife about it.

His Grandparents blessing was what he had hoped for when he came on the course.

I asked why I had cried after the reading and was told it was the emotional feelings being released. Wow!

Another course I did there was on Tarot reading, we spent all the morning and some of the afternoon, learning all about the major and minor Arcana cards. We were all given a new pack of Tarot cards which we could keep.

We were all very excited by this but when I came to pick up and deal the cards I felt extremely ill I told my Tutor and she gave me another pack of new cards, the same thing happened.

I went and made a cup of tea and went into the fresh air, I immediately felt better. But when I went back inside and picked up the cards I again felt very ill, this time a voice inside me said "Tarot is not for you".

When I told my Tutor she immediately gave me a pack of Angel cards and I was fine.

I have always been drawn to Crystals and when I saw a Crystal Healing course advertised I immediately enrolled.

I took some of my favourite crystals with me but these were not needed as the Lady running the class had plenty of crystals there for us to use.

After a morning going through the crystals and their healing powers it was time to try out our healing abilities, I was so excited. Again we each were assigned a partner and a bed to practice on.

My partner asked if she could go first as she needed to lie down, that was fine by me. I walked all around the bed just trying to get a reading off her. I then went over to the crystal table and asked the Angels to guide my hands to the right crystals for the right healing. I selected 5 stones. I lay one stone at her head, one on each side of her waist, one at the bottom of her feet and was told to place the 5th on her etheric heart. I then walked up and down her body with my hands over but not touching her.

As I got to her knees I said to her you have been having a lot of problems here and she said that she had and was unable to bend them very much because of the pain.

I cleared out the blackness in them and then I moved up to her middle area, I just about burnt my hand with the heat coming off her stomach it was red hot. I told her this and she said to me that she had recently had an operation but that it didn't feel right and she was in considerable pain and had nearly cancelled coming to the course that morning, however a voice had told her to go.

I was told to clear it out, which took some time and then I was told to put the crystal from her etherical heart and place it on her stomach for 5 minutes, which I did.

She said that the warmth of my hands was very soothing and took the poison out of her stomach. Her body just seemed to give a sigh of relief.

I hadn't realised that all the other couples had finished and were all standing around watching us, I sat my patient up and the first thing she did when she got off the bed was to do a squat, she said she had not been able to do that for years. She also said that the heat and pain had gone from her stomach she pulled her jumper up and showed us the scar which was a nice thin white line, she told us that earlier this morning her stomach was very swollen and the scar was very red and angry looking.

The Teacher asked me why I had chosen those particular crystals and why I had placed them like I did. I just told her I did as I was told by the Angels, she smiled and told me that I was a very old Healer and was very, very senior in the heavenly realm.

I just do as I am told I said I am only the middle man it is the Angels who send their Healing Powers through me, she just smiled and nodded.

I next went to a Reiki Master to learn Seichem Reiki, I was very excited about this. Reiki is made up of hand movements in patterns. For those who do Reiki it is very effective and a wonderful tool. I couldn't remember the signs I could heal but Reiki and I didn't fit together. The Master told me I didn't need it as I already did it my way.

I believe that you are guided to the path and talents that are yours. Some were not for me Tarot and Reiki, but other forms of healing I know instinctively, like Pranic healing I saw it on television and so I googled it and thought Oh I already know how to do that I just didn't know the name.

I also learnt distance healing funnily enough using a Teddy Bear instead of a human body. My Tutor asked me to do a healing on her Brother who was not very well in hospital. I said to her I was getting feelings of his stomach and throat, they were real hot spots, so I did some cleaning out and put a crystal on both spots.

I was told then that he had throat cancer which had then moved to his bowels which was the heat I felt.

She rang him and asked him how he was feeling he said that he for the first time without his heavy meds he was feeling quite good suddenly and the pain had almost diminished.

My Tutor told him what I had done he was very grateful. BUT you can't heal everyone. People are living their own life path and the serious illness is part of their journey.

Earlier in this book I mentioned that I had gone to live in Western Australia nearer to my 2 daughters.

I was there for 2 years and for me apart from meeting one spiritual lady I found it to be totally barren spiritually for me. My messages stopped coming through even at a retreat weekend at New Norcia Monastry with speakers from assorted religious beliefs. I did not get the spiritual messages I was hoping for.

When I moved to Victoria even though I am isolated on a farm my messages come through loud and clear it is indeed wonderful. On walks birds and butterflies fly around me a wonderful sign.

I have had a new Guide Theodore come through for me and he will stay with me until it is time to take me home. What Bliss.

Since my Awakening I have had a lot people tell me I should heal animals especially dogs, what a beautiful thing helping animals that I love and helping with pain with their aches and pains.

I have also been told I am here to teach people, my comment is usually what would I teach I don't know enough HOWEVER I have found that as you need to do and know something the knowledge is given to you.

As I am a working partner on a Greyhound Property I do quite a lot of healing and massage.

As I write this I am being told that I am to heal dogs, so I will be writing up a plan of action for when I leave here.

Believe me when the Angels want to tell you something they will get through one way or another in other words they "Kick Butt".

HEALING WITH CRYSTALS

Crystals are a very powerful healing agent. I have quite a lot of crystals. Crystals do not have to be large to perform a healing.

If you cannot afford many stones then ask your Angels to help you choose the right stones for the right healings. I find doing this helps a lot.

When you are in a crystal shop TAKE YOUR TIME pick up several crystals of the same type (Until your crystal says pick me) caress it in your hand you will know when it feels right it will blend into your being. Then move onto the next one you want.

Amethyst is a great crystal for meditation it is a calming crystal and for healing it can be used for most problems. It can also be used to clean some of your calmer crystals by laying them on an amethyst cluster. It brings forth calmness and peace.

Carnelian

This stone is an energy stone it can be used for reproductive organs, depression, rheumatism and arthritis

Citrine is an excellent energy stone, it releases negative thoughts and fears, it is also an abundance stone, put a small citrine in your money purse and the money will keep flowing in. A positive stone for all your body as it recharges and helps your energy levels

Angelite

This is one of my personal favourites for healing. Angelite is a healing stone that is good for injuries, it certainly helped me when I dropped a huge piece of wood on my finger which immediately turned black and swelled up to about 5 times its normal size. I held Angelite to it all night it helped with the intense pain and throbbing and kept the blood flow to the wound. It can also be used to balance the physical body with the Angelic realms

Turquoise is a stone that will heal the whole body it is an anti inflammatory and very soothing for the stomach. It was used a lot in the healing processes by the American Indians.

Quartz is the Master Blaster of healing crystals, it can cure any condition, always a must in your armoury.

Smoky Quartz

This stone is wonderful for headaches, cramps, hips, legs and stomachs

Rose Quartz

A very versatile healer helps the chest, lungs, kidneys, soothes burns and increases fertility. It is also very helpful to have a rose quartz and a full glass of water by your computer or telephone to stop energy sapping people.

Lapis Lazuli:

Helps with Migraine headaches and blood pressure, it creates balance and overcomes depression.

It also opens the third eye.

Labradite:

This stone has mystical powers which is shown in the content of make up.

A healer that balances hormones, lowers blood pressure and reduces stress and anxiety.

Also it assist with eye problems.

Black Onyx:

Great for giving peace of mind, holding dreams to the memory and clearing space. especially when you have people constantly in your face.

There are hundreds more excellent crystals out there, plus plenty of books to give you details of not only their healing powers, but also their impact on your chakra's, sun signs and numerology powers that go with the stones.

It is always your choosing to select crystals that resonate with you. Any crystal will work to heal when you call on the Angels to send down their supreme powers to assist you, and always heal for the Highest Good.

When you go to heal make sure you have cleansed your crystals. I place mine in rock salt or sea water, or place them out in the sun for a while. If you are in a hurry you can always ask for the sacred breath and lightly blow on them with the intention of cleansing for the highest good.

I then lay them out and call on the Angels to select the right crystals need for this particular patient, and where to place them for the best result. Remember to ask the Angels to bring the white light of protection down upon you as a protection. You do not want to carry other peoples problems with you.

REMEMBER a Healer is only the intermediary between the Angels and the patient, it is God and the Angels who heal we are merely the vessel.

I have several crystal Angels around my house. And as I was preparing to go to New Zealand for my Fathers 90th birthday followed by my youngest Sisters wedding (to her partner of 10 years.) A lady suddenly appeared to me she pointed at a green Adventurine crystal Angel and asked that I take it with me to give to her son (my Brother in Law to be) she also asked me to tell him that she would be standing with her hand on his shoulder as he got married.

Adventurine is a crystal that is excellent for heart and lungs and other internal organs. As he is a heavy smoker his Mum was doing her bit to protect him.

Both my Sister and Brother-in-Law felt her presence at their wedding.

When I was in New Zealand I had a cousin who I had not seen in years, come to see me, she told me my sister had told her I was psychic and she just wanted to talk to me about it.

Over a cup of tea as we talked about her late Mum, my Aunty (my Dads sister) I suddenly got the smell of a beautiful perfume, I asked my cousin if Aunty had a perfume she always used to wear that people associated with her, she said no Mum wore lots of different perfumes. Then I got the picture of a rose in my mind so I asked if there was a special rose that had something to do with Aunty? My cousin nearly fainted she said that just after her Mother passed she saw a rose called Loving Memory it was highly scented and she bought it as a loving tribute to her Mum. Her Mother also gave me messages that bought great comfort to my cousin, we were both in happy tears at the end of our cup of tea.

I was told to write this book by Arch Angel Michael, he also told me he would get it published.

This book is for those people out there who are suffering in some way or another.

Maybe my story will give you the strength to carry on, to change things for the better.

Please know that there are Angels around you. Let them talk to you, help you and show you love as only they can.

God sends us these wonderful Beings to strengthen us and to help us through the most difficult times.

We can go on in love, we can leave abusive relationships, we can take comfort at the loss of a dear one.

Because this time on Earth is not the journey. The journey starts when we go home again.

Follow your path, walk with Angels, love yourself.

I have been told by Arch Angel Michael that the last incarnation on earth is the hardest journey, Why? Because we need to finalise and atone for previous lives, unfinished business.

Therefore we need to meet people from past lives, who have travelled with us on previous occasions. It may have been a sister who was an uncle in a past life or someone who had made a big impact, but with whom we had unfinished matters to complete. The last incarnation is to say sorry, face up to and finalise our previous life commitments. This does not mean it is a punishment it means when we leave this Earth we are unencumbered, joyous and I guess ecstatic that we are going home to heavenly love.

Oh joy! The weary pathway over

And at last to home we go

The battles have been brutal

But the end result will show

Our Father stands awaiting

A smile upon his face

He says my child it's over

You come home full of Grace.

Namaste.